Ileana Ros-Lehtinen

Lawmaker

Written by Mayra Fernández
Illustrated by Robert Cisneros

MODERN CURRICULUM PRESS

Program Reviewers

Anna M. López, Director,
  Bilingual Education and Foreign
  Languages
  Perth Amboy Public Schools
  Perth Amboy, New Jersey

Kerima Swarz, Instructional Support
  Teacher
  Philadelphia School District
  Philadelphia, Pennsylvania

Eva Teagarden, Bilingual Resource
  Specialist
  Yuba City Unified School District
  Yuba City, California

Gladys White, Bilingual Program
  Manager
  East Baton Rouge Parish School
  Board
  Baton Rouge, Louisiana

MODERN CURRICULUM PRESS

13900 Prospect Road, Cleveland, Ohio 44136

A Paramount Publishing Company

Copyright © 1994 Modern Curriculum Press, Inc.

ISBN 0-8136-5269-3 (Reinforced Binding)   0-8136-5275-8 (Paperback)

Library of Congress Catalog Card Number: 93-79438

Dear Readers,

In this book you will read about the first Hispanic woman to be elected to Congress. When she was a little girl, Ileana Ros-Lehtinen had to leave her native country and come to the U. S. She had to learn English. She studied very hard.

You, too, can be anything you want. Just follow Ileana's example. Read. Study. There are many "firsts" left to be done. Remember that even presidents were once children just like you.

Your friend,

Mayra Fernández

Ileana loved her island home. But in 1959, when she was just seven years old, she and her family left Cuba. They were going to the United States to find freedom.

In Cuba Ileana's parents, Enrique and Amanda Ros, did not have the rights and freedoms they wanted. So they took their family to Miami, Florida, where they could find those freedoms.

In the beginning, life in Florida was hard. Ileana missed Cuba and her friends.

Little by little things got better. Her parents had been right. They found rights they wanted in the United States. Ileana even began to like Miami. The tall palm trees and ocean reminded her of Cuba.

6

At first, Ileana spoke only Spanish.
In the United States she had to learn
English. She was able to learn quickly
in school. When her cousins arrived
from Cuba, she helped them learn
English. She was proud to help.

Ileana was a good student. She
liked learning about the
Constitution of the United States.
She learned that this very important
paper tells about the rights and
freedoms American people have.

Ileana discovered that even as an
immigrant, she had rights, too.
Her parents were very proud that
their daughter had learned all
these new things.

As she studied, Ileana began to dream about what she would be when she grew up. She was very interested in the United States and how it makes its laws.

She even learned by heart the words of President Abraham Lincoln. He said that the United States is a government "of the people, by the people, and for the people."

In 1972, when she was twenty years old, Ileana had one of her proudest moments! She became a citizen of the United States. Now Ileana wanted to do something for this wonderful, new country of hers.

13

First Ileana went to college at
Florida International
University. After she graduated,
she became a teacher and
owner of a private school.

About the same time, she
married Dexter Lehtinen. They
had two daughters, Amanda
and Patricia.

Although she enjoyed teaching, Ileana wanted to serve in the government. She knew she couldn't be President of the United States. The Constitution says you must be born in the United States to be President.

Tallahassee

N
W · E
S

The
Everglades · Miami

Ileana knew there were other jobs she could do. In 1982, she was elected as a lawmaker in Florida.

She did many important things for her state. Ileana helped keep oil drillers out of the Florida wilderness. She also made sure people started to clean up the Miami River.

Laws for the whole country of the United States are made by Congress. Ileana knew there were very few women or Hispanic Americans in Congress. She did not let that stop her. Ileana asked the people of Florida to let her serve there.

In 1989, Ileana Ros-Lehtinen was elected to serve in Congress. She became the first Cuban American woman in that group.

What made Ileana most happy was that the voters of Florida trusted her to make laws for the whole country. She was helping Americans receive the freedoms promised in the Constitution.

Glossary

citizen (sit′ ə zən) A person born in a country or who promises to be loyal to that country

Constitution (kän′ stə too′ shən) **of the United States** The document that lists the rights of Americans and the rules of how the United States will be run

elected (i lekt′ əd) Placed in a job or position because of other people's votes

government (guv′ ərn mənt) All those who help run a country and make the laws

immigrant (im′ ə grənt) A person from one country who arrives to live in another country

About the Author

Mayra Fernández is a teacher in East Los Angeles, California. Dr. Fernández has been teaching for 27 years. She has twelve children, six of whom are adopted. Three of the adopted children are Mexican-American, one is Cuban, one Nicaraguan, and one Pakistani. All form a rainbow of love around her life. Dr. Fernández is kept busy teaching, writing poetry and stories, and giving workshops to parents and teachers. She dedicates this book to Manuel, one of her rainbow children.

About the Illustrator

Robert Cisneros, a graduate in fine arts from the University of Wisconsin, is artist in residence at the United Community Center in Milwaukee, Wisconsin, where he conducts visual arts courses and is curator of the center gallery. His work has been exhibited in the Milwaukee area. Mr. Cisneros has used watercolor to create mural-like illustrations for *Ileana Ros-Lehtinen*.